Jewish Spirituality and Faith

BY
RABBI BERNARD S. RASKAS

W9-AMT-301

KTAV PUBLISHING HOUSE, INC.
HOBOKEN, NJ 07030

Introduction

We live in the presence of spirituality. Spirituality is all around us and in us. Spirituality is a way of looking at the world, thinking about the world, experiencing the world.

Through the lens of spirituality we constantly see the miracle of existence and are inspired to live a meaningful life. In this way we understand that what we daily think and do does matter in the life of the universe. Even more, this approach gives us purpose and faith. It is a faith that strengthens us in adversity and helps us to keep our balance during good fortune.

Through the centuries, Jews have evolved a unique expression of the concept of spirituality. In Jewish literature, history, and other forms, they have expressed their view of spirituality. Using this as a guide, *Jewish Spirituality and Faith* was written.

The thoughts in this pamphlet I expressed originally in expanded form in my three volumes *Heart of Wisdom* published by the United Synagogue of America. I am grateful for their permission to use those books as a source for these writings. It is my prayer that those who read this booklet will find inspiration, hope and comfort in their daily lives.

May spirituality and faith be the condition of all with whom we share the precious gift of life.

Bernard S. Raskas
Saint Paul, Minnesota,
Jerusalem, Israel

Faithfully Yours

We must have faith in ourselves. We do have the ability and the strength to overcome anything that we will have to face. The fact is that we Jews have survived. Equally important is the knowledge that the world has survived.

We should also have faith in God. These are not empty words but the essence of reality. If we are willing to trust life and are willing to trust the processes of the universe, then we ought to trust in God Who is the creator of all existence. This world is our world. We have lived in it and it is part of us. And even if the future is unknowable, there is no reason why we should not enter it with a feeling of trust.

The world is ours. It is rooted in God and we need have no fears. It is important to understand this emotionally as well as intellectually.

Which is the proper path a person should choose? Let one uphold exceedingly faith.

TAMID 28a

Faith Is Doing

It is not enough to feel and to have faith. If we love someone or believe in something, we must be willing to do something about it. This requires effort, determination and active commitment. The scourge of Nazism was not stopped by pious prayers, but by "blood, sweat and tears." The American Jewish community was not built by wishful thinking, but by committees, programs, and hard fundraising undertaken by people who not only believed in the future but were willing to work for it.

If we believe in certain things, we have to be willing to fight for them. Receiving a black eye does not mean we lost the battle; it just means we were willing to fight for our beliefs. If there is any message for us, it is to keep struggling for our commitments. If our goals are still distant, we must not lower our sights, but intensify our efforts. Don't abandon your dreams, hopes and goals. Simply renew them.

The end of faith is but pursuit of truth.

YAAKOV STEINBERG

To Hold With Open Arms

Arguments for the existence of God are almost as numerous as the gods people have invented, but really to know and to feel God requires more than definitions. It is an experience and an achievement that is of the intellect but goes beyond it. The knowledge of God may begin in the crystal clarity of reason, but it ends in the stained glass windows of revelation. Ultimately, we cannot define God, but those who experience God know with a definiteness that transcends all else.

Only with God can we ease the intolerable tension of our existence. For only when the Divine presence is given, can we hold life at once infinitely precious and yet as a thing lightly to be surrendered.

MILTON STEINBERG

The God In You

From our youth through old age, we struggle unceasingly to know and understand God. But God is so vast and many sided that each person sees God in his or her own way, and thus each person, no matter how great, obtains but a glimpse.

The ordinary person sees God plainly and straightforwardly. The more thoughtful individual beholds God in deeper studies and finer meanings. Each in our own way, but each equally valid and true. There is a spark of the Divine in every one of us. How we preserve this spark and pass it on to others clearly reveals the extent to which God is in us. For a spark dies unless it flares into full flame and makes contact with something other than itself.

The soul of a person is the light of God.
PROVERBS 20:27

A Feeling For Faith

The great leaders of Judaism were able to question God and yet maintain their faith. Abraham challenged God (Genesis 18:25): "Shall not the Judge of all the earth do justice?" The Berdichever Rebbe had the courage (or *hutzpah*) to demand that God be brought to judgment because of the way God permitted the Jewish people to suffer. Yet, at the end of his indictment he said: "Magnified and sanctified be the holy name." Elie Wiesel, hurls some powerful accusations against God. Yet his book, *A Beggar in Jerusalem*, is a sensitive affirmation of the presence of God.

All three men shared the ability to live with doubt. They found in their honest faith a strong spur to go on living.

There are mysteries that our reason cannot deal with—pain, death, rapture and ecstasy. It is faith that leads us through these mysteries.

God is concealed from our minds, but revealed in our hearts.

ZOHAR, GENESIS

Judaism In 3-D

We may find Judaism to be more meaningful if we look at it in all three of its dimensions. The first dimension is depth. Our culture goes back thousands of years to almost the first page of history and our ancestors have carved their images upon the heart and conscience of mankind.

The second dimension is breadth. Judaism is a world faith whose adherents occupy every part of our globe.

Judaism excels in the third dimension—height, for it challenges us to reach the heights of human thought and understanding. From our patriarchs through the medieval rabbis to the youngest Jewish child at a biblical lesson, all have found the Torah a mighty stimulus. From every vantage point, Judaism offers a magnificent spiritual vista.

Turn it (the Torah) and turn it over again for everything is in it, and contemplate it, and wax grey and old over it, and stir not from it, for you have no better rule than this.

AVOT 5:25

The Source Of Blessing

On the eighth day of the festival of Sukkot a prayer for rain is included in the service. It expresses our dependence upon Nature and makes us aware of God's daily gifts.

We may plant flowers, but we do not make them grow—God does. In humility we must understand the real source of all creation. And when we desire the blessings of Nature, we do not make them ourselves alone; we must also ask. The energy that is contained in the single seed and the creative powers of a tiny plant that can be released through the droplets of rain bear testimony to a great and provident God.

For You are the Lord our God, Who causes the wind to blow and the rain to descend.

PRAYER INTRODUCED INTO THE DAILY SERVICE ON SHEMINI ATZERET.

Throwaways

We are living in an age of "disposables." Not only tin cans but almost all kinds of utensils are made to be thrown away after use.

But there is a different and more serious kind of "throwaway living" today. People are throwing away moral convictions and principles that are needed for essential living. We cannot dispose of our religious and moral heritage to suit our particular convenience.

Actually this is the basic distinction between a materialistic and a religious outlook. Materialism seeks satisfactions from living through the world of things. In the spiritual approach, material acquisitions are valuable only insofar as they advance the life of spirit. Things are to be used and not loved. On the other hand, people and ideals are to be loved and not used.

Be not like servants who serve their master upon the condition of receiving a reward; but be like servants who serve their master without receiving a reward; and let the reverence for Heaven be upon you.

AVOT 1:3

Days Are Scrolls

The most basic problem of humanity is not educational but spiritual. The human mind does not need to be stuffed, it just needs to be opened—opened to the wonders of living. Life leaps up like a geyser for those who drill through the rock of indifference, inertia and insensitivity.

This search for life also should be the essential purpose of all our prayers. Prayer is not a statement of human greeds but an honest expression of human needs. We should not pray, "Help me to win!" but rather, "Help me to live!"—to live and forgive, to live and believe, to live and give, to live and love.

Babies become great human beings only by striving and living creatively. It is within our power to make our lives great. For this reason hope and faith fill our hearts; confidence and trust possess our minds; cheer and goodwill dominate our spirits.

Days are scrolls: write on them what you want to be remembered.

BAHYA IBN PAKUDA

The Meaning of Courage

Moses has an experience at the Burning Bush and is given the charge of leading his people into freedom. The Bible records the reaction of the Hebrew slaves: "And they did not listen to Moses because of shortness of breath and hard labor" (Exodus 6:9).

However, one may interpret the verse: "They did not listen to Moses because of shortness of spirit." They didn't have faith in God, faith in Moses and, most important of all, faith in themselves.

Israel is no exception to this rule. Because the pioneers drained the swamps and fertilized the desert they were able to lay the foundation of a state. The following generations built on that foundation. The strength and success of Israel today flows from its citizens' and its supporters' faith in the face of seemingly insufferable difficulties.

If we want to achieve something worthwhile, we must be willing to have faith in ourselves despite setbacks and obstacles.

Courage is never to let your actions be influenced by your fears.

ARTHUR KOESTLER

14

It Is Up To You

All of us all day long, as we face ourselves and as we face the world, have the opportunity to increase our well-being. It is so simple. One word of praise can make all the difference in the world. As it is written in Proverbs 16:24: "Encouraging words are as honey, sweet to the soul, and health to the being." A teacher's word can make or break a student. A parent's praise can lift or drop a child. An employer's judgment can be given gently or caustically. These things are very real and very important. All of them come out of a choice and a faith. Faith in one's self and faith in others, choosing a way of being that celebrates life—these make happy and productive human beings.

We must constantly emphasize the positive and eliminate the negative. Negative feelings frustrate, deny and destroy. Positive expressions help the individual to realize himself and affirm the meaning of life.

I call heaven and earth to witness this day: I have put before you life and death, blessing and curse. Choose life that you and your offspring may live.

DEUTERONOMY 30:19

It's Risky

Faith means risking. Faith means trust in God and ourselves. Ultimately faith is something we do in spite of the consequence.

If we have an ideal or a value and if we are willing to keep faith with it, we will eventually achieve something fine, glowing and wondrous. It could be in a career or in a business. It could be in a cause for others. But the important thing to realize is that our achievement will be tested by the depth of our faith. The challenge comes not in the beginning when it is easy but in the middle when it is tedious and difficult. But those who believe in themselves and their values will find that the risk was worthwhile.

Faith is not a series of theorems but a way of life.

SHMUEL HOGO BERGMAN

On A Note of Hope

Prayer serves to instill a sense of hope. Although far from perfect, the world is a good world with many possibilities. So when we are faced with a challenge, why assume the worst? Why not hope for the best?

After all, despite centuries of defamation and persecution, we Jews are flourishing. Many civilizations have vanished without a trace, but Judaism is alive and well. Despite problems and pressures, we are coping and we are succeeding. We may have questions, we may have doubts, but we know that God is great and God is good.

One of the most beautiful prayers in the *amidah* is "We give thanks." And the prayer ends with some of the most moving words in the human language: "We have always hoped in you." It is a fact that "Where there is life, there is hope."

Hope is the sun shining upon the life of a person.

MOSHE LEIB LILIENBLUM

17

Leave A Little To God

Very often we forget the implication of the phrase that the world is a unity. It means simply that there is a purpose and destiny in the world.

Solomon Schechter, the second president of The Jewish Theological Seminary of America, used to say repeatedly, "Leave a little to God." Note that he did not say: "Leave it all to God," for then we become nothing, or "Leave nothing to God," for then we are doomed to failure. We must do our share and know that God will too. We must work and wait.

What will emerge will be in accordance with God's purposes for the world—not Russia's or America's, or yours or mine, but something far different, far better than what we possess at present. For humanity was created in the image of God and what God does imagine will be the future. The world is a unity, that is why we must work and wait, and leave a little to God.

God who has created the day has also created sustenance for it.

MEKHILTA, BESHALAH

The Lost Art

We are so busy talking to God that we cannot hear what He has to say. If we pray merely to talk and not to listen, we miss the meaning of worship. Prayer is dialogue with God; it is conversation with the Almighty. It is common knowledge that the best partner in a conversation is the one who is the best listener.

God is not a cosmic bellhop whom we call in to attend to our needs. God is not a person and God cannot be fooled or deceived. People scan the face, but only God knows the heart. We must not promise that which we cannot keep. We must not ask for that which cannot be given. We must be cautious in our speech and even more patient in our silence. We must learn the art of listening in order to learn.

Humans were endowed with two ears and one tongue that they may listen more than speak.

SHEM TOV FALAQUERA

Wake Up

"And Jacob awaked out of his sleep, and he said: 'Surely the Lord is in this place; and I knew it not' " (Genesis 28:16).

There are times in our lives when we seem to be walking through life in a dream-like stroll and suddenly we are startled by an event and we become aware of God.

During rites of passage—birth, adolescence, marriage, parenthood, death—we are suddenly made aware that life is greater and vaster, and we are moved to contemplate the powerful forces that move our lives. In our good fortune or our misfortune, we understand how much we depend on others. We realize the immenseness and the complexity of a harmonious universe. These events also make us realize that we are in the presence of God.

Wherever you go, God goes with you.
DEVARIM RABBAH 2:10

The Constant Miracle

We usually think of miracles as instances in which the natural course of events is interrupted and changed. Actually, miracles are constantly occurring around and within us, miracles that give us more cause for inspiration and faith than we ordinarily perceive.

The Talmud tells that the daily healing of the sick is greater than the biblical report that three men passed through a fiery furnace unharmed. The daily miracle of the body's healthy functioning is more wondrous than the unique instances of miraculous recovery.

Every time we experience the smooth working of nature, we see revealed the miraculous providence of God. In this essential goodness can be apprehended the true miracle of existence.

Our whole program of Jewish living is to help us to become articulate and express our wonder as we stand in awe before God.

ABRAHAM E. HALPERN

No Comparison

Whenever we think of God, we must be aware that we are exploring a mystery; and when we have exhausted our thought, we have moved but one small fraction closer to comprehending God. Our lifetime is as a split second against the earth's eight billion years. We stand upon approximately two square feet in a universe that is described by a number with twenty-four ciphers in it. We grow humble and begin to perceive that are but specks of dust.

Such thoughts stir us greatly. How, we wonder, can an individual stand on the hills and gaze at the stars, walk by the seashore and hear the endless pounding of the surf, look at a newborn infant and not understand that there is a God? And what that God thinks of us is far more important than what we think of God.

To whom will you liken God?
And to what can you compare the Eternal.

ISAIAH 40:18

Partners

There is a fundamental relationship between God and people in the management of the world. This relationship is one of cooperation. That is to say that we literally co-operate or jointly take action with God.

The laws of the universe were created for the fulfillment of our function and destiny. When we begin to look upon life from this perspective, we learn to make full use of natural and moral resources for our own welfare. In their obedience comes our co-operation with the divine scheme for the universe.

Judaism has a central, unique and tremendous idea that is utterly original—the idea that God and humans are partners in the world and that, for the realization of God's plan and the complete articulation of this play upon earth, God needs a committed, dedicated group of men and women.

THEODORE GASTER

Time On Our Hands

The giant sequoia trees have endured for centuries. This is because they take a great deal of time to reach their full growth.

Similarly, we must understand that it takes time to develop *our* spiritual strength and to reach *our* maturity. Certain things simply cannot be hurried. It takes nine months to develop a healthy baby. There are twenty-four hours in a day and no force on earth can hurry or delay that cycle. It takes *shivah*, a full week, for a mourner to accept the fact of a death; *sheloshim*, a full month, to accept the loss; and *avaylut*, a full year, to adjust to the deep pain. And no pill or scheme can shorten these periods.

That is why we should have time on our minds rather than time on our hands.

The Hebrews affirm the reality and importance of time. To them, it was not an illusion, something from which one must escape, but something which must be redeemed.

JAMES PHILLIP HYATT

Reason and Ritual

Many of us often lose sight of the real value of religion. We become so laden down with ritual that we forget that the fundamental purpose of a ritual is to express a relationship with God. Ritual serves as one of the bridges between us and God and must always be seen as such. Ritual is never an end in itself, but always the means to a greater end. Therefore, every ritual must be performed with understanding. When ritual is mechanical it defeats its purpose, but when it is sincerely practiced and its proper function understood it becomes the finest link between people and God.

God considers not only the form of the worship, but also its sincerity.

ME'IL TZEDAKAH 346

Trial By Fate

Those who have deep convictions about living deeply, fully and meaningfully are totally unconcerned about death. They firmly believe that a person, who has a soul and was created in the image of God, has a role and a purpose on this earth. What it is we can never be entirely certain, but one of the ways we can live in faith is to live with fortitude.

As we grow older, we learn that not everything in life can be cured; some things we must learn to endure. To dare is great, but to bear is even greater, for bravery we share with brutes, but fortitude and endurance with saints.

There is no limit to trials, but the wise learn thereby.

SOLOMON IBN GABIROL

The Opiate Of The Masses

Whether we admit it or not, we are all involved in deep religious feelings. There are times when, because of group or personal rebellion, we find ourselves hostile to the idea of God, but then in our unguarded moments, we let slip through our authentic feelings. There is not one person who does not at some time struggle with conscience about the mystery of existence. Even those who insist they do not believe in God show by their very vehemence that they are concerned about God's existence.

God is an undeniable part of our lives, and ultimately we cannot live in peace with ourselves until we are prepared to accept this. We may scribble anti-religious slogans on the walls, but when we find that a crisis has passed, we still pause and say humbly, "Thank God."

The Eternal is not the God of would-be-spirits—but the God of the human heart.

HAYIM NAHMAN BIALIK

Wrong Problem

It is a characteristic inversion, so typical of our times, to speak of the "problem of God." At stake in any real discussion about God is rather the "problem of being human." We are problem, but God is solution. Trouble occurs whenever we confuse one with the other.

How would you feel if God gave us the same amount of attention as we devote to the Divine Presence? If God offered as many excuses as we do, and if the excuses were no more justifiable than ours? If God withheld blessings from us as we withhold our offerings from God? The next time you are asked to do something, to give something, stop to ask yourself, "What would God have me do?"

You depend on God, not God on you.
                                    BAHYA IBN PAKUDAH

By Way of Chicago

No one really possesses a pipeline to God and no one faith has a corner on the market of Heaven. To think in these terms is to distort the function of religion.

Religion does not seek the detailed will of God in any given time and place, for the fundamental function of religion is to discover the basic teachings of ethical truth. Religion does not communicate to us the specifics of life, but rather its broad principles from which we derive a way of conduct. The search for moral perfection is not an easy task and there is no absolutely safe and certain path. The paradox of religion is that God is in every person's heart, and yet no one can know God fully.

Revelation is the silent, imperceptible manifestation of God in history. It is the still small voice.

HERBERT M. LOEWE

The Big Flash

Following the first atomic explosion in New Mexico, observers were discussing what had gone through their minds when the "big flash" came. Dr. J. Robert Oppenheimer thought of a line of Sanskrit: "I have become Death, Destroyer of worlds." But William L. Laurence, the science reporter for the *New York Times*, said quietly that he thought, "This is the kind of a flash when the Lord said, 'Let there be light.' "

Tomorrow at dawn there will flash the first light for the new day. People will gather to welcome the first daylight with prayer and contemplation. We have hope because of the light of love, understanding, mercy, and truth. This is the only true light that can illuminate our world with faith and confidence.

The Holy One, observed, "How long shall the world exist in darkness? Let the light enter!" And God said, "Let there be light."

GENESIS RABBAH, CHAPTER 1

The Faith Behind "Amen"

The Hebrew term for faith is *emunah*. *Emunah* is quickly recognizable in the more common form of *ahmayn* or *amen*. It was first used by Psalmists and is still part of the prayer structure of the religions of the western world.

When we say "amen," we are in fact affirming our faith in God. We are demonstrating our willingness to accept the ways of the world, even though at any given moment they may not be so pleasing. It is a willingness to suspend judgment until we have greater perception, greater experience and greater knowledge.

If one lives in good faith with God, one will accept all events as a part of life. It is no great feat to accept a relationship when it is easy and profitable. But it is something to fulfill the terms of a relationship when it taxes and wearies us. Faith on a full stomach may be simply contentment; but if you have it when you are hungry, it is genuine.

Wait for the Lord; be strong, take courage, and wait for the Eternal.

PSALMS 27:14

Polished Religion

Only when we establish a habit of celebrating customs and holidays can religion have real meaning for us. When we observe the time-tested rituals of Judaism we keep open the channels of communication with God. Every time we participate sincerely in a ritual, we renew our faith.

When a young boy ascends the pulpit and reads the Haftorah, he reactivates his faith. When a young woman kindles the Sabbath candles, she reactivates her faith. And when we stand at the graveside of a dear one and, overwhelmed with grief, utter the words, *Yitgadal veyitkadash shemay rabba*, "Sanctified and magnified be the great name," we reactivate our faith in God and the world. Experiences like these give us the inspiration to carry on and the strength to endure.

Religion will not come to our aid the moment we call; it must be loved and cherished at all times if it is to prove our true friend in need.

GUSTAVE GOTTHEIL

Faith Is Not A Blindfold

Faith can never be a substitute for the responsibilities of life. Faith can only do so much and the rest must be accomplished by skill, training, work and study which, of course, are based on a faith in a good and provident God.

Faith is not something we believe in spite of the evidence; it is something we do in spite of the consequence. Faith tears the blindfold from our eyes and forces us to see injustice when we would prefer a life of ease. True faith does not permit us to remain complacent and calm in the face of evil.

Albert Schweitzer has expressed this simply: "No one may shut his or her eyes and think that the pain which is therefore invisible is non-existent. No one may escape responsibility."

Serving God and humankind, through the inspiration and instrument of faith, forces us to involve ourselves, to give of ourselves, and if need be to offer up our lives.

It is not incumbent upon you to complete the work, But neither are you free from doing all you possibly can.

AVOT 2:21

The Sum Is All The Parts

Religion, if it is to have any value at all, must be practiced every day, hour and minute. When religion is sealed off from involvement in the concerns and affairs of people and the concrete particularity of daily decisions, it becomes sterile and meaningless. If our faith is to function, we must allow it to grapple with our pressing personal problems.

Every day is a messenger of God. God places choices before us daily so that we can never isolate ourselves from ethical issues. Those who sit in seclusion or dodge issues or think they will find salvation by a few pious words are sadly mistaken.

We cannot rise to God by stepping on the heads of others. We cannot hate during the week and love God on Saturday or Sunday. Religion is the sum of *all* its parts.

People must beware of looking upon religion as an ideal to be yearned for; it should be an ideal to be applied.

SIMON DUBNOW

Does God Believe in You?

We may well ask, where is God found today? The answer is that the God Who entered the huts of Pharaoh's slaves in Egypt is working for freedom and opportunity in the ghettos today. The God Who spoke at Sinai to Moses is the God Who is with the Israel of today. The God Who spoke to Adam and told him that all people are one is the same God working in the world councils through people who are willing to take every setback and every devious dealing and still persevere in their work for peace and harmony. God will always appear where people of good will, of good faith, and good hope will let God in—or better still—let God work through them.

And so the ultimate question is not, do you believe in God? But, does God believe in you?

"You are My witnesses that I am God" (Isaiah 43:12). When you are My witnesses, I am God; when you are not My witnesses, I am—as it were—not God.

MIDRASH TEHILLIM 123:2

A Thinking Person's Religion

Those of us who seek religious integrity realize that it isn't just an emergency hatch to be used when disaster strikes. To be of real use in time of trouble, prayer must have become a regular and disciplined part of our lives long before there was trouble.

There is no such thing as faith at first sight. The one who is swift to believe is swift to forget.

For this reason we must earn our faith every day. To be of value religion must be used constantly. It is pitiful to encounter a "cardiac Jew," one who assures us and himself with, "I am a good Jew at heart." This is an emotional cover-up for a lack of thinking. What we really need is a "cerebral Jew," one who can say, "I am a good Jew in my head." We must not be taken in by nostalgia and sentimentality. We must develop a religion of thought and intelligence that will offer guidance, inspiration and hope.

A humble person walks on earth, yet his or her thoughts reach the sky.

SAMUEL HANAGID

The Pillars Of Prayer

The heart of prayer is not how many words we say, but rather the spirit in which we say them. Prayer is not a marathon in which the one who has said the most is necessarily the one who has done the best. Nor is it a speech contest in which the one who pronounces the words the most clearly is the winner. Prayer is an edifice built on the pillars of sincerity, conviction and trust in God, people and the universe.

Prayer must rest on a faith and a firm conviction in its purpose and its value. We must believe what we say, we must believe what we pray—or our prayer becomes mechanical, if not downright hypocritical.

My words fly up; my thoughts remain below:
Words without thoughts never to heaven go.
WILLIAM SHAKESPEARE

A Person Is Not Alone

The Bible tells us, "Isaac sowed in the land and reaped a hundredfold the same year and the Lord blessed him" (Genesis 26:12). There is a hundredfold increase because people and God are working together. That we need God, we already know. But here God also needs us. Real progress is made when both forces operate in harmony.

God stores the hills with marble, but it takes a Michelangelo to sculpt a statue. God stocks the forests with wood, but it takes a Stradivarius to make a violin. God blesses human beings with abundance. Where they use nature wisely, it is with restraint.

Ultimately, the destiny of the world is in our own hands. It is not enough to pray; we have to take action to build a better world.

Therefore we pray to You instead, O God,
For strength, determination and will power,
To do what we can,
To do what we must,
Then we will find our reward a
hundredfold. . . .

JACK RIEMER

Belonging

All of us need to feel at home in the world, and for the religious person this sense of belonging demands a close and warm relationship with God. People whose philosophy of life includes a simple but personal relationship with God live with a feeling of security. When we know we belong to God and God belongs to us, we can surmount every obstacle and deal effectively with the problems and challenges we must inevitably face.

When we relate to God, then we know that we belong in the deepest sense possible.

Where can I escape from Your spirit?
Where can I flee from Your presence?
If I ascend to heaven, You are there;
If I descend to Sheol, You are there too.
If I take wing with the dawn
To come to rest on the western horizon,
Even there Your hand will guide me,
Your right hand will hold me fast.

PSALMS 139:7–10

The Path Through The Forest

The Hebrew word for Jewish law is *halakhah* and it comes from the root *halokh*, meaning "to go." So *halakhah* means literally "a path." Faith, with all of its laws, rituals and ceremonies, provides a well-worn path to guide us through the maze of life. Our rules and observances are not arbitrary, but are the results of wisdom wrung out of the experience of thousands of years.

The Sabbath comes once a week and tells us not that we *can* rest but that we *must* rest. By placing the *mezuzah* on the door of the home, we do not nail a magic charm on the entrance of a house but rather do we say that a home is a sacred place and a family is a religious unit.

If we did not have rituals of faith, we would quickly descend into chaos.

The halakhah does not deny any emotion, it guides it.

HAYIM NAHMAN BIALIK

Tomorrow Is Only A Day Away

Commenting on the verse "Taste and see that the ways of the Lord are good" (Psalms 34:9), the rabbis ask how it is possible for everything we experience to be good. Their answer is that it is in our power to find something positive in everything that happens to us. We must make up our minds that events and encounters in the coming year will make us stronger, wiser, more caring, more loving human beings. No matter what befalls us, we must have faith—faith in ourselves and in tomorrow.

Today is merely a bridge to tomorrow.

FRANZ ROSENZWEIG

Worship Without Words

Judaism is essentially a faith based on deed rather than on creed. This unique concept of worship without words finds appropriate expression in a classic Jewish story.

Rabbi Israel Salanter, the founder of the modern Jewish ethics movement, once failed to appear in the synagogue on Kol Nidre Eve. His congregation waited, then became worried and went out to search for him. After several hours they found him in a neighbor's barn. On the way to the synagogue Rabbi Salanter had found a neighbor's calf which had strayed and become entangled in the brush. With great difficulty he tenderly freed it and brought it back to the barn to tend its wounds.

They protested, "How could you do that? Don't you know that your first duty as a rabbi is prayer?"

He answered gently, "God is called *Rahmana*, the Merciful One. An act of mercy is a prayer, too."

It is not external ritual that wins forgiveness, but inward sincerity.

TAANIT 16a

The Source Of Light

Jacques Lipschitz, the sculptor, spent his youth in Paris. One day a painter complained that he was dissatisfied with the light he painted and went off to Morocco, seeking a change. He found that the light in his Moroccan canvases was no different. Lipschitz then told him, "An artist's light comes from within, not from without."

Even as we are all artists in life, we must strive to kindle the light within. All that we touch and feel only serves as a stimulus. The true creative spark lies within our heart and soul.

We must learn to kindle our inner spiritual light. We can do this by developing the ability to trust ourselves and our own judgments. The nurturing of the inner spiritual fire is a lifetime enterprise. We must follow that light wherever it leads us.

The light of a candle is serviceable only when it precedes one on the way, useless when it trails behind.

BAHYA BEN ASHER

A Modern Aladdin's Lamp

Many of us still approach prayer in an immature fashion. We think of prayer as magic, just as we think of God as being a heavenly magician. We pray selfishly: "O Lord, make my business prosper; grant me recovery from illness; give me relief from pain; save my dear one." But we do not pray, "Help me to accept the reality of life and to face the truth to live on with courage and dignity."

In Greek the word for prayer is *eychomai*, "to wish"; in German it is *gebet*, which is rooted in the verb "to beg"; but in Hebrew it is *tefilah*, which means "to be judged." Prayer is a way of standing before God and accepting with equanimity what life has to offer us. Prayer helps us to live with truth, for truth is God.

For I have come to know your truth;
I accept your judgments upon me
And am content with my life.

THE DEAD SEA SCROLLS

The Untouchables

Ultimately, the stars symbolize the everlasting presence of religion and God among us. If every religious mark and symbol were to disappear, the stars would still remain as reminders of the everlasting nature of the universe, the timelessness of religious values, and the source of all life.

We must always remember this lesson in dealing with the daily issues of life. We must always abide and cherish the deep feeling that certain values are unshakable and certain religious convictions are untouchable. There are certain teachings that are lofty and claim our ultimate loyalty. These truths remain with us and give us the strength to meet the difficulties of life and to resolve them. For as the stars are untouchable and everlasting, so is the essence of God.

Lift up your eyes on high and see who created these. Then to whom will you compare Me, says the Holy One.

ISAIAH 40:25–26

Gam Zu Letovah

The great Akiba ben Joseph distilled his faith into a formula: *Gam zu letovah*, "Whatever God does is for the best."

Once while Akiba was on a mission to Rome, he and his group came to a city and found all the inns filled. They were forced to sleep in a field. They had with them a donkey, a rooster, and a lantern. During the night, the wind extinguished the light, a fox carried off the rooster and the donkey was killed by a lion. Akiba awoke and simply remarked, "It is for the best."

The next day, they found the city in ruins. Invaders had sacked it. Akiba said, "Had we found accommodations in the city, had light been burning in the field, had the donkey brayed or the rooster crowed, we would not be alive. My friends, it is always *gam zu letovah*."

All my life I have been waiting for the moment when I might truly fulfill the commandments. I have always loved the Lord with all my might and with all my heart; now I know that I love God with all my life.

AKIBA BEN JOSEPH

You Are More Than You Are

We often wonder what effect our conduct and our religious faith have upon others. An interesting example can be found in a true story gleaned from the Talmud.

Simeon, the son of Shatah, sent his pupils to buy a camel from an Arab. When they brought him the animal, they gleefully announced that they had found a precious jewel in its collar. "Did the seller know of this?" he asked. When they said he did not, Simeon retorted, "Return the gem to the Arab immediately."

When the heathen received it he exclaimed, "Blessed be the God of Simeon ben Shatah. Blessed be the God of Israel!" This exclamation was dearer to Simeon than all the riches of the world.

In everything we say and do, we must remember that to others we represent the living image of our faith.

A person is always responsible for one's actions, whether awake or asleep.

BAVA KAMMA 3b

As A Mighty Stream

An ancient Talmudic teaching, whose lesson is especially meaningful in our time, reads: "The Torah is compared to two paths, one of fire and one of ice. If a man turns to one, he will be burned, if he turns to the other, he will be frozen. What shall he do? Let him walk in the middle."

This is one of the finest insights our tradition can offer us into our own position with regard to the past and the future. The true function of religion is to combine a vast awareness of the past with a deep sense of the future.

We must maintain a steadfast loyalty toward our faith, but at the same time be willing to experiment, and thereby permit the living waters of Judaism to flow surely and serenely. In order for Judaism to live, it must flow between the frozen ways of static faith and the fires that indiscriminately destroy the values of the past.

The old must be renewed, and the new must be made holy.

ABRAHAM ISAAC KOOK

Without Measure

By having the right kind of faith in God and in people, we can change the destiny of humankind. The ultimate in human tragedy is not suffering or even death, but despair. People have been known to suffer all manner of torments and to maintain a deep and abiding interest in life, a sense that life is worth living. Martyrs, like Akiba and Socrates, have gone to their deaths with serenity because they believed that their death was not the final verdict on all they lived for.

All religious faiths require us to believe unequivocally that we can change the course of our personal lives and thus the lives of all humanity.

The recognition of a person's innate dignity as God's co-worker is basic to a proper understanding of one's nature, as manifested in one's creative ability, one's moral responsibility, and one's untapped potentialities.

ROBERT GORDIS

Near You

One of the most basic ways a parent can reassure a child is simply by saying, "I am here." The presence of a loving person is the deepest source of reassurance.

The religious equivalent of this is "God is here," or even "God is." The idea of God as a presence is the most meaningful concept in the entire galaxy of human feelings. When a person accepts this idea in perfect faith, then tension, anxiety, and fear are assuaged.

God is near to us: as close as the whisper of the heart, as omnipresent as the air we breathe. To summon God, we need not shout; we need only whisper the thought "God is near."

God is near unto all who call upon the Eternal,
To all who call upon God in truth.

PSALMS 145:18

The Need To Grow

A disciple once asked the Baal Shem, "Why is it that even one who clings to God and knows he is close to the Eternal sometimes experiences a sense of interruption and remoteness?"

The Baal Shem explained, "When a father sets out to teach his little son to walk, he stands in front of him and holds his two hands on either side of the child so that he cannot fall, and the boy goes toward his father between his father's hands. But the moment he is close, his father moves away a little and holds his hands farther apart; the father does this over and over so that the child may learn to walk."

The significance of this analogy is that God encourages us to walk and that the world welcomes us with open arms. To grow in knowledge and understanding of life is the most rewarding of all experiences, for we never outgrow the need to grow.

God is subtle, but not malicious.

ALBERT EINSTEIN

Training Ourselves To Love

True love, like real maturity, begins to grow when your concern for someone else outweighs your concern for yourself. Instead of taking, love means really giving— giving money, time and emotional commitment. Think for a moment: what does a parent do for the love of a child, and what does a child do for the love of a parent? And the love between mates, how much do they strain to pay the price of their love? And what do we sometimes have to do in our love for America and for Israel, and for humanity at large? Finally, are we really prepared to accept the efforts and the struggles involved in expressing our love for God?

It is not really easy to love God or even to love another person. It takes tenacity, it takes faith, it takes responsibility.

Training through love breeds love.

WILHELM STEKEL

The Natural Law

In Judaism, naturalness and directness have always been dominant themes. The naming of a child at birth involves only a simple prayer. The Jewish marriage ceremony itself is modest in length. Even in death, Jewish practices and the burial service have always been simple and direct. Those who add to the length of the services do so on their own for their own needs, but that is not the way of traditional Judaism. In the Sefardic Jewish community it is the tradition to have a tombstone that lies flat on the ground so that no one can try to show superiority by boasting of a bigger and better monument. Naturalness, unpretentiousness/ and directness are the Jewish ways.

The higher the truth, the more natural it is.
                                        ABRAHAM ISAAC KOOK

Make An Offer

An offering is not truly worthy unless it be accompanied by the passion of a willing heart. Religion teaches us that the main gift is the sincerity of the offering and the depth of the feeling that accompanies it. Unless we can give freely and openly, the gift is as naught.

In 1561 an Italian rabbi named Raphael Norzi wrote *Marpay Lanefesh*, "the healing of the soul." In it the medieval rabbi said: "Anything done in sincerity and reverence of God, though it have nothing to do with Torah, will ensure us eternal life."

Therefore, each of us must search in his or her own heart; whether, our prayer be offered twice a day, once a week, or even once a month, it must be prayed with the whole heart. Nothing less is acceptable.

The Lord spoke to Moses saying, "Speak to the children of Israel that they make offerings, and accept an offering from every person whose heart so moves."

EXODUS 25:2

Time To Stop

The ultimate defeat of fear comes about through faith: Faith in ourselves that we can solve our problems and faith in God that God has given us the resources and the hope to solve those problems. Faith is not a magical device, but rather a sure scale against which to measure our fears. If fears are to be resolved, they must be seen in the perspective of a good God, a helpful society and a friendly universe.

Four decades ago, a great American President said, "The only thing we have to fear is fear itself."

Three centuries ago, a great New England governor said, "Here we feared a fear where there was no fear."

Over two millennia ago, a great Hebrew prophet said: "Fear not, nor be anxious for I am with you, for I am Your God" (Isaiah 41:10).

You shall not be afraid of the terror by night, nor of the arrow that flies by day.

PSALMS 91:5

The Still Small Voice

In our increasingly noisy world there is an increasing need for quiet. Great periods of development and growth usually come not with crushing intensity but rather with calm quiet. Consider the flowers. Do they push their way up from the earth noisily, or is their work done in silence?

Einstein once indicated that the heart of religion is "to wonder and stand rapt in thought." And Moses lived on the mountain for forty days and nights alone in meditation before he came down with the Ten Commandments. From these two men of genius we can learn that creative social thought requires quiet. It is in the quiet recesses of the soul that we make our important decisions. So, true religion is not noise but rather a silence and an inwardness that precedes the taking of public stands and the making of commitments.

And God was in the still small voice.

I KINGS 19:11–13

Wait A Minute

Before we do anything we first ought to stop and think about God. This is particularly so in terms of the good things in life. In trouble and in anguish we turn to God, but so often we forget about God in pleasure and in plenty. The Bible tells us that upon good fortune, we should remember to pause and express our gratitude.

Prayer is one thing that distinguishes a human being from an animal. Upon coming home and finding the family healthy and safe, one expresses thanks to the Almighty. A person who is blessed with material possessions does not take them all for granted but lets his or her gratitude speak for him or her.

The first step of all wisdom is reverence for the Lord.

PROVERBS 9:10

The Evidence of God

We can neither prove nor disprove the existence of a Supreme Being. For every argument on one side, one can find an equally convincing argument on the other side. Ultimately, faith cannot be completely demonstrated. It is not illogical; but, on the other hand, it cannot be proven absolutely either. It is simply that as you live and experience and think and feel, you either know in the very marrow of your bones that there is a God, or you do not.

As a house is impossible without a builder, a dress without a weaver, a door without a carpenter, so the world cannot be without a Creator.

MIDRASH TEMURAH, CHAPTER 13

Here And Now

The Ten Commandments are very lofty, yet they are couched in general terms. Judaism in its method and its wisdom applies these ideals in specific ways. The Torah portion each week leaves the lofty heights of Sinai and brings the moral law down to the valley of daily decision. For example, the Bible gives us a detailed analysis of the laws of interest, a specific description of what constitutes false testimony and gossip, and even the laws on responsibility for property loss through fire, neglect and so on.

We tend to think that religion belongs in a synagogue or a church—a House of God. But isn't a home were morality is practiced also a House of God?

Religion will serve its true function when it enters the experience of our daily lives. We tend to associate religious thought with heaven, when we really should understand that morality belongs to the here and now.

Better one hour of repentance and good deeds in this world than all the life in the world to come.

AVOT 4:22

Cheers

We all have problems, we all have pressures, and we are perpetually beset by challenging situations. But our faith teaches us that despite it all, we must hold fast and make the most of life at any age.

A young man reported that when his grandfather was in his eighties, he would get up every morning, look at the newspaper, have one quick drink of liquor, and then sit down to breakfast. One day the grandson asked, "*Zayde*, why do you start the day looking at the newspaper, having a drink, and then having breakfast?"

The answer came as follows: "*Mein kind* (My child), I get up in the morning and I open the newspaper to the obituary page. If I don't see my name, then I take a drink and say '*Lechayim*' (to life)!"

We must retain our zest for living. God gave each of us the gift of life. What we do with this life is our gift to God.

Happy is the person who finds wisdom, and the one who obtains understanding.

PROVERBS 3:13

On The Rise

We should approach God not only through intellect but also through feelings, not only with our minds but with our hearts. Our prayers should be uttered not only as words, but as an expression of emotion.

A rabbi observed a man mumbling in the synagogue and asked, "Can you pray?" "No." Then the rabbi asked, "What did you do during the Days of Awe?"

"Rabbi," the man said, "I only know the letters from *alef* to *yud*. When I saw how intently everybody was praying, my heart broke. Then I began to recite *"Alef, bet,* and so on. After that I said, 'Lord, take these letters, turn them into words, combine them, and may they rise before You as a sweet scent!' That is what I said with all my strength, over and over." The rabbi said, "This man's prayer is more worthy than all the hymns in the prayer book."

Do not think that the words of prayer, as you say them, go up to God. It is not the words that ascend; it is rather the burning desire of your heart. . . .

ARTHUR GREEN

Footprints

A man dreamed he was walking along the beach with the Lord. Across the sky flashed his life. For each scene he noticed two sets of footprints in the sand. Then he noticed that many times there was only one set of footprints. This happened during the lowest times in his life.

He questioned, "Lord, You said that once I decided to follow You, You would walk all the way, but during the most troublesome times of my life, there was only one set of footprints. When I needed You most, You deserted me."

The Lord replied, "My precious, precious child, when you see only one set of footprints, it is because then I am carrying you."

In our pain we do not notice that we are carried by the love of God as well as the love of family and friends. We are sustained and strengthened by many support systems until we can once more walk safely and securely.

For God will order angels to guard you wherever you go. They will carry you in their hands.
PSALMS 91:11–12

Everywhere Or Nowhere

The Bible tells us what to eat and what not to eat. It contains instructions on how we are to dress. It even discusses the uses of fire. We may think that these are unlikely topics for a religious text. For what does God have to do with food or drink or clothes or the use of the natural elements? The answer is: Everything! The truth of the matter is that God is everywhere or God is nowhere.

This, then, is one of the meanings of religion. God is not to be worshipped merely one day a week, on our so-called official day of rest. God is with us all the time. God is with us everywhere.

God is in all things and out of them; above all things and beneath them; before all things and after them.

PLANTARIUS

Building Bridges

The Kaddish prayer is written in Aramaic. It has not one reference to death and yet it is the most significant prayer during mourning, *yahrzeit* and *yizkor*. Often before people recite the Kaddish there is anguish and disorientation. But as soon as we finish, we usually find a mood of relaxation and acceptance. It is not the content that is significant but the sounds, the rhythm and the attitude.

One of the purposes of religion is to help us during the crisis points of our lives. Birth, adolescence, marriage, illness and death bring fundamental changes. In order to bridge those changes we literally have to build bridges.

It is important to have forms that will provide us with the means of transition so that we can go peacefully through life.

Out of divine commandments and deeds we build our bridges.

SONG OF SONGS RABBAH 8:10

Spirits

"Not by power, nor by might, but by My spirit, says the Lord of Hosts" (Zechariah 4:6).

Why did the Rabbis choose this verse to epitomize Hanukkah? Judah Maccabee was a war hero. The Maccabees won by force. The history of the events seems to indicate just the opposite of this verse.

If we consider that period in history, however, we will find that spirit was the ultimate determining factor. Indeed, had not the Maccabees been infused with the spirit of freedom and devotion to Judaism, they would never have had the strength and the courage to keep fighting. When there is spirit, there is strength; when there is no spirit, a cause vanishes like smoke on a windy day.

A pure heart create for me, O God, and renew a steadfast spirit within me.

PSALMS 51:12

Tradition Is A Bridge

In the Jewish way of life, convictions and beliefs are bound together by customs, ceremonies and celebrations. The ceremonies enable each generation of Jews to hand over the teachings of tradition to the next generation.

The Passover Seder is not merely a family meal, but a way to ensure that the ideal of freedom will continue. Shavuot is a means to restate the moral law and to teach that Sinai touches every day of our lives. Rosh Hashanah tells us that life is not just random, but is endowed with meaning and purpose. Yom Kippur teaches us that we are tempted not because we are evil, but because we are human.

Birth with a Hebrew blessing, Bar or Bat Mitzvah with a prophetic reading, marriage with a huppah, death with the recitation of *kaddish*—the customs make up the tradition that tells us who we are and what we must do.

From the Jewish heritage, I have derived my world outlook, a God-centered interpretation of reality in the light of which man the individual is clothed with dignity.

MILTON STEINBERG

Pray Tell

Prayer is our instinctive reaction to the world, to fears and hopes, frustrations and dreams, strivings toward self-realization.

The Bible teaches that anyone can pray. This should not be taken for granted. Prayer was often the prerogative of the few. Among pagan cults there were prayer texts that no one could utter but the priest in the temple.

But in the Bible we find a whole new approach. Any place, it tells us, is a proper place in which to pray to God. The Bible teaches that religion is carried in the heart and is not bound to any shrine or relic.

Moreover, Biblical prayer is the honest expression of the sensitive soul, not a set incantation. Beginning with the experience of Moses at the burning bush, Jewish tradition breaks with magical rites and superstition. All a person need do is think of God, and he or she is in the Divine Presence.

Prayer, if offered from the heart and for the sake of heaven, ascends on high and pierces the firmament.

OR YESHARIM

The Real Way

We often wonder about what is the real way to find the meaning of religion. Many times the direction is misguided. Religion is not to be found only in a book or a building, for it is a way of life. True, the book may be a source for thought and the building an inspiration, but both are valueless unless they help people to live better lives. Religion is the response of the soul to that truth. A person who is really religious will think and live and act indicating his or her belief in God's existence, as if the Ten Commandments were a part of one's daily life, as if truth and honesty were more important than life itself. That person will have an overpowering yearning and desire to live with the real meaning of religion.

To the question, "Where is God?" the Kotsker rebbe replied simply, "Where God is admitted."
HASIDIC LORE

A Growing Wonder

Religion should not be unreasonable, nor need it ever contradict the laws of logic. Religion itself undergoes evolution and growth and, if it is deeply sensitive, it is always sifting and refining.

Similarly, in our own thinking about God, we must understand that as we grow we must discard our childish notions about God, without discarding God Himself. A mature faith means a growing and expanding vision of God. Some of us still pray to an elderly gentleman in the sky, instead of learning to grow in religious knowledge and accept new concepts and shed useless thoughts.

At every stage of life, we must be willing to learn more about God, because the more we see of God the greater the Almighty appears to us. Faith is, indeed, growing wonder.

And so they serve the Creator by doing commandments of reason, and by good spiritual conduct; and by these things they add to the known commandments.

BAHYA IBN PAKUDAH

Trust Yourself

Maurice Friedman, the philosopher, described our contemporary needs well when he said, "What modern man needs is not 'faith' in the traditional sense of that term, but a life stance on which to stand and from which to go out and meet the ever-changing realities and absurdities of our technological age."

This is an important insight into our world today. We are staggered by the rapidity of events. It seems the rules of the game of life are always being changed. This constant revision sets us running off in all directions seeking the magic solution: gurus, cults, and charismatic leaders; only believe and ye will be saved.

But we eventually tire of these experiments. The solution to our problem, the ability to cope with our concerns, lies within our own way of life, in our very own hearts. We have to learn to trust our own traditions and our own best instincts.

Abraham, the first patriarch, drew moral force from himself and walked in righteousness by his own effort.

RASHI ON GENESIS 6:9

Breakthrough

The Exodus from Egypt was a Divine turning point in history which decisively altered our concepts of God, humans and society. God intervened in the events of history and redeemed the Children of Israel from slavery. They were liberated from the spiritual bondage of idolatry and paganism; they were also liberated physically from persecution and oppression. The Exodus from Egypt is not simply a past event, but is a living encounter with the Divine Presence. It commits us to struggle against idolatry, injustice and oppression in every generation. Time and again, when it would appear that we are at the brink of oblivion, we emerge defiant, victorious through our own effort and the will of God.

Faith gives us the substance of our values and ideals and sustains us with the belief that they will be realized.

In every generation there are those who rise up against us seeking to destory us, but the Holy One, may He be praised, delivers us from their hands.

HAGGADAH

71

Good Taste

A ritual, a ceremonial or a religious function often works in a specific fashion, tapping a reservoir of chemicals in the brain known as "endorphins." A sip of wine on Friday night, a piece of *matzah* on Pesah, honey on Rosh Hashanah, *latkes* on Hanukkah, *hamantaschen* on Purim are Jewish stimuli. When we taste them they release certain substances within us that are pleasing. These tastes strengthen and relax us in very real ways.

Many years ago a bright college student came to the campus minister and said, "Religion is only a crutch." The minister replied with a smile, "And who isn't limping these days!"

The stresses of life necessitate that we take every opportunity to help us bear the inevitable strains that wear us down.

Taste and see that the ways of the Lord are good.
PSALMS 34:9

Prayer Is Practical

Prayer relieves anxieties. Prayer gives us a sense of perspective, enabling us to measure our lives against a set of values. Prayer identifies us with our people. Prayer connects us with the vast resources of our tradition to help us deal both with failure and success. Prayer is an opportunity to voice our pain in times of sorrow and to express thanksgiving in moments of joy. The purpose of prayer is threefold: helping us to accept things as they are, maintaining a sense of balance, inspiring hope in the future.

Prayer helps us to help ourselves. It enables us to use the wisdom of the ages to our best advantage. We can truly say that prayer has practical consequences. It helps us to live more stable and tranquil lives.

If a person must travel on the highway, he should offer a threefold prayer: the regular prayer, a prayer for a safe journey, and a prayer for safe return.

MIDRASH HANEELAM

Patches On Our Souls

Religion endeavors to teach us to rise above the material cares of this world and be concerned instead with the meaning of our lives. We are constantly being asked in our prayer books to reconsider who we are, what we are, and why we are. We ask to be forgiven, even as we pledge ourselves to forgive others. We ask to be loved, even as we commit ourselves here and now to love others. We ask to return in faith perfect and true, even as we are sure that understanding and mercy await us.

One of the great purposes of religion is to train us to think in terms of values and people rather than in terms of possessions and things.

Return unto Me, and I will return unto you.
MALACHI 3:7

God Is In Us

In the Book of Genesis we read, "And God appeared to Abraham." The questions we might ask are, did God appear only to Abraham and to no one else? Where does God appear? How does God appear? And, indeed, where is God in our time?

This age-old question was raised in the class of a well-known rabbi. A student asked, "Rabbi, where does God dwell?" The rabbi thought for a moment and then replied, "God dwells wherever people let the Divine Presence in."

God is all about us, and is with us whenever we choose to let God in. If we do not act as though there were a God in the world, then there is no God in the world. But if we act as if God were real, then the Almighty really is here. The validity of this approach can be proved not from books or writings, but only from life itself.

The Lord is with you while you are with the Eternal.

II CHRONICLES 15:2

The Rest

The *Shabbat* ritual is the high point of Jewish thought. For *Shabbat* is the real answer to paganism. Paganism proclaims that days must be spent in drive for power and that people are animals. *Shabbat* presumes time is holy and people are sacred. Paganism admonishes that might makes right. *Shabbat* advises that strife is the enemy of life and the the peace of the Sabbath—*Shabbat shalom*—is life's greatest boon.

The entire system of rituals of the *Shabbat* is designed as help to control our lives so that its false and pagan values do not get out of hand to overwhelm us. To prevent our reversion into a modern paganism, we must hold fast to those forms and values that help us to remain civilized and sensitive human beings.

The law of the Sabbath is the essence of the doctrine of ethical monotheism. It is the epitome of the love of God.

HERMANN COHEN

Where God Is Revealed

Prayer is one activity that distinguishes human beings from animals. The Psalms, in their sublime beauty, celebrate birth and marriage, suffering and death, the wonders of nature, the just society.

Most of us think that a miracle is a one-time thing that occurs in a stupendous way. Actually, this is not so. There is hardly a moment when we cannot see a miracle if we want to. The real miracle is what happens to us every day of our lives: The miracle of creation! The miracle of a healthy body that functions so normally and serves us so ably! The miracle of nature that brings forth through seeds and seasons all the glories of our universe!

Revelation is the silent, imperceptible manifestation of God in history. It is the still, small voice; it is the inevitability, the regularity of nature.

HERBERT LOEWE

As Old As The Hills

The Jewish experience is as old as the hills. This implies stability and strength, knowledge and wisdom, faith and reassurance. Psalm 121, one of the oldest Psalms, was probably written by a Jewish pilgrim thousands of years ago as he approached the Hills of Judea. He looked forward to visiting the Temple in Jerusalem and he prayed: "I lift up my eyes to the hills [and I ask,] 'What is the source of my help?' My help comes from the Lord, Creator of heaven and earth."

It behooves us to remember the grandeur of the universe and the possibilities the Creator has bestowed upon us. We ought to recall the rhythms of nature and the fact that there are ebbs and flows in the affairs of people as well. Anxiety is inevitable. We must not act as if we were immune to all the fear and trembling that is a natural part of the human condition. God does not ask us not to feel anxious, but to trust in the Almighty no matter how we feel.

Faith is devotion to God.

JACOB JOSEPH KATZ

A House For God?

If we want God to dwell among us, we have to make room. Sometimes we become so involved in the world we forget to summon the presence of God. To hear the call of God, one must be within listening distance. To neglect régular attendance at a House of God is to break an appointment with God. To forget to perform the *mitzvot*, the daily good deeds, amounts to canceling a contract with God.

The problem that we have in making God real is that we still cherish the notions about God that we acquired as children. But God is not a place, a person, or a promise—God is a presence! God is very real and very near to those who want the Divine Presence.

God does not die on the day when we cease to believe in a personal deity, but we die on the day when our lives cease to be illuminated by the steady radiance, renewed daily, of a wonder, the source of which is beyond all reason.

DAG HAMMARSKJOLD

More Light And Less Heat

The roof of the *sukkah* must be made of leaves or branches, with openings wide enough so that one can see the light of the sun by day or the stars by night. No heat but plenty of light. Perhaps this is a way of telling us that we need less of the heat of anger and tension; more of the light of understanding and tolerance.

Tolerance is not an admission of weakness but a mark of strength. When a person is intolerant of other views, he is merely saying that he is afraid of exposing himself to the possibility that others might have some truth on their side. When we are strong in our faith we have no need to be apprehensive of those who disagree with us; we may even be able to say, "While my approach seems right for me, your way may be right for you."

If we develop tolerance, we can take the stresses of conflicting views with serene confidence.

A wise person's duty is to be scrupulously faithful to the religious laws of the country and not to abuse those of others.

JOSEPHUS

Every Little Tree

We can learn a lot from trees. A typical apple tree will produce one hundred thousand leaves and an elm tree six million, no two of them exactly alike. An apple orchard of one acre will collect and discharge 480 tons of water a month. Just think how trees quietly contribute to the shaping of our natural world. One learns from this example that the most powerful forces in the world are not necessarily accompanied by noise and obvious change, but rather silence and subtlety.

We often talk about God and wonder where God is. Did God really create the world? What is God's power? When these questions come to us we might think about trees. Is it possible that a tree with its simplicity and yet with all of its complexity could be an accident of nature? The world and all of its harmony surely cannot be the product of chance.

The tree speaks to us of God's handiwork in all the world.

The power of nature is the power of God.

BARUCH SPINOZA

Save This

The seventh day of the festival of Sukkot is known as Hoshana Rabbah, "the great saving." Yom Kippur is the day of atonement, but so great is the compassion of God that if there are any sins left to be forgiven they can be redeemed on Hoshana Rabbah. It is a way of saying that the gates of mercy are never closed.

The principle behind Hoshana Rabbah represents a very important insight into human nature. We do not suddenly turn over a new leaf. It takes time and patience to develop a new orientation and to withdraw from old habits. Hoshana Rabbah is highly realistic. It says to us: Never despair. If you took two steps forward yesterday and you fell one step back today, you are still ahead by one. A mistake is only a mistake, it is not the final defeat.

Open the door of repentance only the width of the eye of a needle and God will open it wide enough for carriages and wagons to pass through.

SONG OF SONGS RABBAH, CHAPTER 5

The Bedrock

Religion is an important and established institution. While organized religion has changed and will have to change even further to keep up with new insights into the nature of humanity and the meaning of God, we must still hold fast to the basic traditions that strengthen us and guide us in our search for the good life. If the roots of religion are torn out, then the tree of faith will shrivel and die, and with it will perish the great moral and ethical teachings which have evolved over the centuries. If this happens, what will take its place?

The basic function of traditional religion is to keep society ethical and stable. That is why religion as an institution must be kept intact while at the same time we try to breathe into it new direction, energy and relevance.

Blessed is he who keeps the foundation of the ancestors.

II ENOCH 52:9

An Expression of Joy

Every person in his or her relationship with God should consider the moral law and religious observance not as a burden, but rather as a joy and an opportunity for fulfillment. When we do not do what we should have done, we feel anxiety. But when we have fulfilled what was asked of us, or what we ask of ourselves, we feel relaxed and happy.

In talking of contributing to important causes, we often take a distorted view. We say, "Give until it hurts." What we should really say is, "Give until it feels good."

A passage in the writings of the Baal Shem Tov, the founder of the Hasidic movement, states this concept exactly: "It is the aim and essence of my pilgrimage on earth to show my family by living demonstration how one may serve God with merriment and rejoicing. For one who is full of joy is full of love for people and one's fellow creatures."

You shall rejoice before the Lord your God.
DEUTERONOMY 16:11

Healing Through Encounter

In France a doctor has worked for many years among the poor. He is now a very old man but continues to serve faithfully. One day an elderly woman watched him as he skillfully bandaged the wound of her grandchild. After several minutes she said, "Doctor, you have treated three generations of my family and you have perfected the art of healing." The wise old doctor replied, "Thank you, but I only dress the wounds; God does the healing."

This is the true relationship between people and God. Our responsibility is to dress the wounds of suffering that exist about us, and through God, healing will be effected.

All we need do is dress the wounds, and as they heal, we ourselves will be healed in turn. The mystery of healing is that the one who applies the dressing as well as the one who receives the balm is healed.

Heal us, O Lord, and we shall be healed.
                                    DAILY SERVICE

Deep Are The Roots

Learning itself does not suffice unless it is anchored in fundamental convictions about using it for the proper purposes. Learning itself, without applying it to the enhancement of one's spiritual life and the betterment of society, can be vain and useless. We need roots to give us that kind of support that will anchor our wisdom to meaning and worth. Life is not an aimless pursuit of distraction; it has very definite purposes. These purposes are revealed by the articles of faith that give us a continuing source from which to draw inspiration and strength.

Unless we have the roots that give us the proper hold on life, we become like the tumbleweed, which drifts and wanders aimlessly, driven by every wind.

Let not your wisdom exceed your deeds
Lest you be like a tree with many branches and few roots.

AVOT 3:22

The Presence of God

Each of us in our own way knows there is a God, and it is unimportant whether we know the Eternal's name or not. Our spirit cannot be deceived, our own inner feelings are the surest guide toward great spiritual truths.

We stand in God's presence and we know the Eternal is here as we live in the world God created. We experience God's presence when we view the soaring majesty of the heavens or a bird in flight, appreciate the fragrance of a flower or the warmth of a friend's hand, gaze up at a distant mountain or down at a smiling infant, feel the cool breeze of a summer night and the warm love of one's beloved. All this expresses the reality of God which is a link between us and the universe through the bond of faith.

Religious experience is an attitude of oneness not only in oneself, not only with one's fellow humans, but with all life and, beyond that, with the universe.

ERICH FROMM

So Big

We ought never to have a static concept of God. If we are religiously mature, our view of God is constantly expanding.

When you ask a youngster, "How big is the baby?" the child smiles, stretches his tiny arms and says, "So big." His arms are small and so is his comprehension. We hope that as he grows, so will his understanding spread.

It is also this way when it comes to thinking about God. When we are children, our idea of God is "so big"—small and limited by our dearth of experience. In adolescence, our view of God is "so big"—somewhat wider, but yet restricted by our not having experienced the fullness of life. Then as we reach maturity our concept of God should be high, wide and deep, unlimited in its scope and expanse. Our experience in living should enable us to stretch our arms and our minds to their farthest reaches.

I have set the Lord always before me.

PSALMS 16:8

A Person Is Not Alone

When an airplane approaches a landing a signalling device indicates when the plane is too distant from the mark. This indispensable device also gives the pilot a great deal of confidence.

This is also true of our approach to God. The instrument of conscience flashes when we are wide of the mark of morality. In any period of stress we are never alone.

Elijah heard the still, small voice in the desert. Socrates admitted that all that was worthwhile in his life was due to the guidance of an inner angel. Epictetus, the stoic, expressed the position of all religions: "When you have shut your doors and darkened your room, remember never to say you are alone, for you are not alone, but God is within."

Longing, I sought Your presence
Lord, with my whole heart did I call and pray,
And going out toward You,
I found You coming to me on the way.

YEHUDAH HALEVI

I Am A Hebrew

The special character of the Jew is the concern with preserving a direct relationship with God that stands as the focal point of all existence.

Consider, for example, that other faiths have their names compounded with a founder or savior: Buddhism is the religion of Prince Gautama Buddha; Christianity is based on the name of its founder. But Judaism refers simply to the religion of the Jew. The Jew fervently maintains that between humans and God there is no need for an intercessor. The relation between the moral world, the natural world, God, and humanities is one. There is but one God, the God of all people and all creation.

I am a Hebrew; and I fear the Lord, the God of heaven, who hath made the sea and the dry land.

JONAH 1:9

Keep Your Feet On The Ground

Judaism flourishes today because it has met the test of history. One of the reasons for Judaism's spiritual strength is that it has been exposed to every philosophical test and has stood its ground.

Mahatma Gandhi once said: "I want the cultures of all the lands to be blown about my house as freely as possible, but I refuse to be blown off my feet by any of them."

The modern American Jew, like this great Indian seer, must be open to all points of view while holding steadfastly to his or her own faith. We must help the many causes in our wider community, but we will first accept our responsibilities to the Jewish community. We will look at the changes wrought by modern life, but we will also look to the wisdom of the ages before we change our devotion to Jewish life.

The greatest honor I can give my children is love for our people, loyalty to self.

THEODOR HERZL

In A Word

The words we say most often are usually the words we think about least. We constantly use words without being aware of their deeper meanings. For example, many self-proclaimed atheists are not aware that every time they utter a goodbye, they are really saying, "God be with you."

One word which is most commonly used throughout the world is truly the least known of all. It is the most popular word in the Christian, Jewish and Muslim services: "Amen." We use it so often in our services, but rarely stop to consider what it really means. Literally, "Amen" means something like "It is true" or "I affirm." Its source is the Hebrew word *"emunah,"* which means faith. It is also close to the word *"ne'eman,"* which means firm and trusting. The uttering of this word is, therefore, in itself an act of faith.

The person who says "Amen" sincerely is counted as if the entire prayer had been said.
SHULHAN ARUKH, ORAH HAYIM 124:1

The Orderly Universe

We do not often pause to contemplate the fact that the order of the universe reveals the presence of God. The solar system is perfect in its arrangement; the sun rises and sets at its appointed hour; and in general nature functions with absolute precision. The discovery of miracle drugs is founded on research which in turn is based on fixed mathematical principles of an orderly universe. The precision and the power of the laws and forces of the universe daily declare the reality of an intelligent God.

The sensitive mind does not see a conflict between science and religion, but rather a cooperative effort in which each discipline helps the other; the scientific study of religion and the religious study of science can help us live better lives.

A little science estranges men from God,
Much science leads them back to the Almighty.
                                        LOUIS PASTEUR

First Things First

How deep are your convictions about God? Is your attachment like a rubber band, pulling toward the Almighty under pressure, but then releasing God when there is lassitude?

The owner of a large shoe manufacturing firm in St. Louis has the following motto framed on his office wall: "God first, others second, shoes third." I have often wondered what would happen if we all adopted this motto with deep personal commitment.

There would be no war, for we would say, "God first, humanity second, and arms third."

Family quarrels would disappear, for we would say, "God first, relatives second, and jealousy third."

Many of our tensions would vanish, for we would say, "God first, others second, and my drives third."

When we truly believe in God, we put first things first.

All that the Creator demands is that a person make a beginning in the right direction; thereafter God will aid him to continue on the right path.

REB NOAH LEKHIVITZER

How Deep Are Your Roots?

Once a young student came to Rabbi Akiba and said, "Teach me about faith." Rabbi Akiba showed him a tiny sprout and said, "Pull it up." The young man did so quite easily. Then the sage told him to pull up a young sapling. The lad did it with just a little more effort. Then he asked the boy to remove a small shrub from the earth. With both hands the young man did so. Finally, the rabbi asked him to uproot a full-grown tree. The student pulled with all his might but could not even shake a leaf. And Rabbi Akiba said, "Just so, my son, is it with faith. If our roots are deep, if our religion is grown and mature, no one can uproot it. Remember this, your faith will always be as strong and as powerful as are your roots."

Roots demand cultivation and nurturing. Faith, in a similar manner, requires our constant tending through study, thought and periodic recommitment.

The stronghold of the wicked crumbles like clay,
But the root of the righteous bears fruit.

PROVERBS 12:12

The Way To Worship

Hymns, music and words are all necessary to worship, but that which is truly indispensable is a certain frame of mind, an attitude of sincerity. We must understand that everything else is a form of embellishment; sincerity is the heart of the matter. For it is only the honest heart that can enter into a dialogue with God.

We cannot step on people's heads and hope to raise ourselves to God. We cannot be dishonest and think that God will look into our hearts with blessing. We cannot hope to win God over with flattery and smooth words. God is beyond all this, for God is absolute truth. One need not go to outer space or even to the great outdoors to find God, for the Almighty is to be felt right in the sanctuary of our own hearts. But if we do not have the right attitude, the proper spirit, then the Eternal will never appear to us anywhere.

Sincerity is a prerequisite of worship.

DAVID OF TOLNA